100% 백점 맞는 영어습관

초등필수 영어동화

따라쓰기 ⑤

Little Red Riding Hood 빨간 모자

Cinderella 신데렐라

백점 맞는 영어습관
초등필수 영어동화 따라쓰기 ❺

초판2쇄 발행 | 2020년 1월 20일

지 은 이 | WG Contents Group
발 행 인 | 정현순
발 행 처 | 지혜정원

출판등록 | 2010년 1월 5일 제 313-2010-3호
주   소 | 서울시 광진구 천호대로 109길 59
연 락 처 | 02-6401-5510
팩   스 | 02-6969-9737
홈페이지 | http://www.jungwonbook.com

디 자 인 | 정원재
그   림 | 주정원, 박지영

ISBN 978-89-94886-28-2 64740
      978-89-94886-22-0 (세트)

값 9,500원

100% 백점 맞는 영어습관

초등필수 영어동화 따라쓰기 ⑤

WG Contents Group 저 | 주정원, 박지영 그림

지혜정원

초등필수 영어동화 따라쓰기의 효과

① 손을 많이 움직이면 기억력과 이해력이 증가합니다.

영어동화를 읽어야 한다는 필요성은 알고 있지만 접근하기가 쉽지 않은 것이 사실입니다. 그리고 단순히 쓰기만 한다고 아이들의 실력이 늘까 걱정이 되기도 합니다. 중요한 것은 처음부터 무리해서 많은 양을 쓰도록 욕심내지 말아야 한다는 것입니다. 아이의 성장은 비단 영어실력만이 아니라 모든 것이 느려 보이기도 합니다. 하지만 아이는 매 순간 정신적, 육체적으로 성장하고 있으며 영어 또한 그러한 성장과 마찬가지로 꾸준히 성장하고 있습니다.

손은 제2의 뇌라고 하고 발은 제2의 심장이라고 합니다. 손을 많이 움직이면 그만큼 기억력과 이해력을 증가시킬 수 있습니다. 영어 단어나 문장을 단순히 읽기만 했을 때와 따라쓰기 했을 때의 차이는 큽니다.

② 긴 문장을 읽고 쓰는 것이 쉬워집니다.

영어로 무언가를 읽고 쓸 때는 아이가 흥미 있어 하는 것부터 시작해야 지루하지 않게 오래 지속할 수가 있습니다. 그런 의미에서 아이들이 좋아하는 쉬운 영어동화책부터 시작한다면 책을 읽고 따라 써 보면서 영어 공부 뿐 아니라 생각의 폭까지 넓어지는 장점이 있습니다. 처음에는 그냥 그림과 함께 읽어보고 한 문장 한 문장 따라쓰다 보면 긴 문장을 읽고 쓰는 것이 쉬워집니다. 그리고 전체 스토리 뿐 아니라 문장 하나하나까지 음미할 수 있는 날이 오게 됩니다. 영어동화를 따라쓰면서 많은 생각을 하게 되므로 생각의 크기도 커집니다.

 ## ③ 쓰기에 자신감이 생깁니다.

영어 학습의 주된 목표는 의사 소통입니다. 그리고 영어 학습에서 중요한 것은 반복과 꾸준한 노출이라는 것도 이미 많은 분들이 잘 알고 있습니다. 영어 읽기, 듣기, 말하기도 중요하지만 쓰기를 통한 학습 또한 중요합니다. 실제로 영어를 공부하는 사람들이 가장 어려움을 느끼고, 실력 향상이 힘든 것이 바로 쓰기라고 합니다. 하지만 이렇게 어려운 쓰기를 재미있게 할 수 있는 방법이 있다면 아이가 흥미를 느끼게 되고 자연스럽게 쓰기 실력도 늘게 되지요. 실력이 늘면 자신감 또한 늘어나게 됩니다. 그리고 자신감이 생기면 아이는 따라쓰기 뿐 아니라 자신의 생각까지 자연스럽게 영어로 쓰게 됩니다.

Contents

Story 1

Little Red Riding Hood
빨간 모자

Story 2

Cinderella
신데렐라

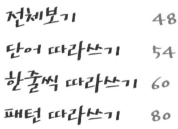

My Book Report   85
나만의 독서록 쓰기

책의 특징

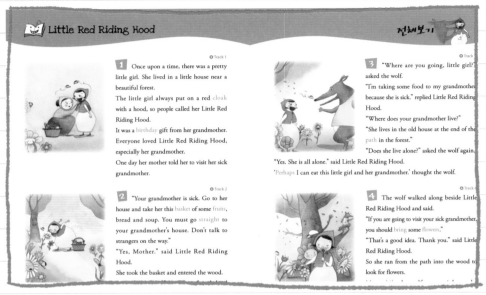

전체보기

영어명작동화를 전체적으로 소리내어 큰 소리로 읽어봅니다.
MP3를 먼저 듣고 읽어봐도 좋습니다. 단어 따라쓰기에서 나오는 단어는 빨간색으로
표시해서 미리 볼 수 있도록 하였습니다.

단어 따라쓰기

동화에서 나온 꼭 기억해야 할 단어들
을 따라 써 봅니다.

패턴 따라쓰기

필수패턴을 따라쓰고 그 패턴을 활용한
문장을 보고 생각하며 글을 써 봅니다.

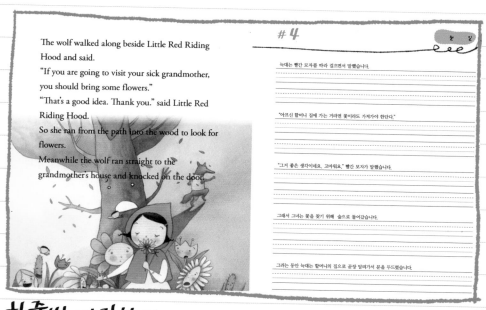

The wolf walked along beside Little Red Riding Hood and said.

"If you are going to visit your sick grandmother, you should bring some flowers."

"That's a good idea. Thank you." said Little Red Riding Hood.

So she ran from the path into the wood to look for flowers.

Meanwhile the wolf ran straight to the grandmother's house and knocked on the door.

4

늑대는 빨간 모자를 따라 걸으면서 말했습니다.

"아프신 할머니 집에 가는 거라면 꽃이라도 가져가야 한단다."

"그거 좋은 생각이네요. 고마워요." 빨간 모자가 말했습니다.

그래서 그녀는 꽃을 찾기 위해 숲으로 들어갔습니다.

그러는 동안 늑대는 할머니의 집으로 곧장 달려가서 문을 두드렸습니다.

한줄씩 따라쓰기

영어동화를 재미있는 그림과 함께 넣었고 필수패턴은 바로 알아볼 수 있도록 색을 넣어 표시했습니다. 동화를 읽고 한 줄씩 따라 써 봅니다.

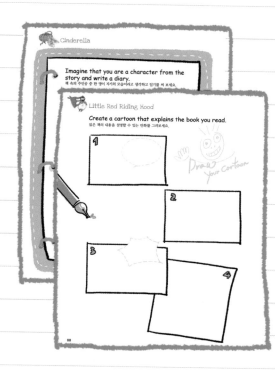

나만의 독서록 쓰기

이야기를 모두 읽고 따라쓴 후 나만의 독후활동을 해 봅니다. 지시에 따라 그림을 그리고 요약하면서 자연스럽게 동화의 내용을 복습해 볼 수 있습니다.

MP3 파일 다운로드

www.jungwonbook.com에서 MP3 파일을 다운받아 활용하세요. 동화 스토리를 생생하게 들을 수 있습니다.

Story 1

Little Red Riding Hood

빨간 모자

Little Red Riding Hood

1 Once upon a time, there was a pretty little girl. She lived in a little house near a beautiful forest.

The little girl always put on a red cloak with a hood, so people called her Little Red Riding Hood.

It was a birthday gift from her grandmother. Everyone loved Little Red Riding Hood, especially her grandmother.

One day her mother told her to visit her sick grandmother.

2 "Your grandmother is sick. Go to her house and take her this basket of some fruits, bread and soup. You must go straight to your grandmother's house. Don't talk to strangers on the way."

"Yes, Mother." said Little Red Riding Hood. She took the basket and entered the wood. Suddenly a big wolf stepped out from behind a tree.

Track 3

3 "Where are you going, little girl?" asked the wolf.

"I'm taking some food to my grandmother because she is sick." replied Little Red Riding Hood.

"Where does your grandmother live?"

"She lives in the old house at the end of the path in the forest."

"Does she live alone?" asked the wolf again.

"Yes. She is all alone." said Little Red Riding Hood.

'Perhaps I can eat this little girl and her grandmother.' thought the wolf.

Track 4

4 The wolf walked along beside Little Red Riding Hood and said.

"If you are going to visit your sick grandmother, you should bring some flowers."

"That's a good idea. Thank you." said Little Red Riding Hood.

So she ran from the path into the wood to look for flowers.

Meanwhile the wolf ran straight to the grandmother's house and knocked on the door.

Little Red Riding Hood

◉ Track 5

5 "Who's there?" asked the grandmother. "It's Little Red Riding Hood, grandmother." answered the wolf, making his voice as soft as he could.

"Oh, come in sweetie." The grandmother opened the door and was eaten by the wolf. He put on the grandmother's clothes and hid in her bed.

When Little Red Riding Hood had gathered so many that she could carry no more, she remembered her grandmother.

She ran back to the road, and soon she came to her grandmother's house.

◉ Track 6

6 "Hello, grandmother." said Little Red Riding Hood. "I've brought you some food, and some beautiful flowers!"

Little Red Riding Hood looked at her grandmother. "You must have been real sick. You look very strange today."

Little Red Riding Hood came closer to the bed.

"Oh, grandmother, what big ears you have!"

"All the better to hear with, my child." the wolf responded.

7 "What big eyes you have!" she said.

"All the better to see with, my child."

"But grandmother, what big teeth you have!"

"All the better to eat you up with."

Before the wolf finished those words, he jumped out of bed and gobbled up Little Red Riding Hood.

He was now so full and sleepy after both Little Red Riding Hood and her grandmother.

He climbed back into the bed and fell asleep.

8 The wolf was snoring very loudly.

A hunter passing by heard his snoring.

'I've never heard the old woman snore that loudly.' he thought.

So the hunter went into the house.

As he entered the bedroom, he found the wolf in grandmother's bed.

"Oh no! The old woman must have been eaten by the wolf."

Track 9

9 Just then he could hear the people crying for help inside the wolf.

"Somebody, help! Somebody, help!"

The hunter cut the wolf's belly open.

Little red riding hood and grandmother climbed out off the wolf.

"Thank you so much." they said.

Little Red Riding Hood ran outside and picked up lots of stones.

The hunter put them in the wolf's belly and the grandmother sewed the belly up.

10 Then the wolf woke up.

"I am very thirsty. I wonder why I feel so heavy."

The fat wolf went to the pond to drink water.

He bowed to drink water, but he fell in the pond.

Little Red Riding Hood, her grandmother, and the hunter
were delighted.

And Little Red Riding Hood was always careful not to talk to
any strangers.

cloak   cloak   cloak   cloak   cloak   cloak

망토

birthday   birthday   birthday   birthday

생일

basket   basket   basket   basket   basket

바구니

fruit   fruit   fruit   fruit   fruit   fruit

과일

straight   straight   straight   straight   straight

똑바로

stranger stranger stranger stranger stranger
낯선 사람

suddenly suddenly suddenly suddenly
갑자기

path path path path path path path
길

perhaps perhaps perhaps perhaps perhaps
아마

bring bring bring bring bring bring
가져오다

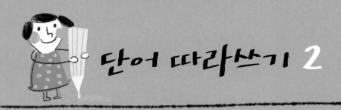

단어 따라쓰기 2

flower flower flower flower flower flower

꽃

meanwhile meanwhile meanwhile meanwhile

그 동안에

voice voice voice voice voice voice

목소리

clothes clothes clothes clothes clothes

옷

gather gather gather gather gather

모으다

remember remember remember remember

기억하다

sick sick sick sick sick sick sick sick

아픈

respond respond respond respond respond

대답하다

gobble gobble gobble gobble gobble

게걸스럽게 먹다

sleepy sleepy sleepy sleepy sleepy sleepy

졸리운

snoring snoring snoring snoring snoring

코고는 소리

hunter hunter hunter hunter hunter hunter

사냥꾼

bedroom bedroom bedroom bedroom

침실

hear hear hear hear hear hear hear

듣다

belly belly belly belly belly belly belly

배

sew   sew   sew   sew   sew   sew   sew   sew

바느질하다

wake   wake   wake   wake   wake   wake   wake

(잠에서) 깨다

thirsty   thirsty   thirsty   thirsty   thirsty

목이 마른

heavy   heavy   heavy   heavy   heavy   heavy

무거운

delighted   delighted   delighted   delighted

아주 기뻐하는

Little Red Riding Hood

빨간 모자

Once upon a time, there was a pretty little girl. She lived in a little house near a beautiful forest. The little girl always put on a red cloak with a hood, so people called her Little Red Riding Hood. It was a birthday gift from her grandmother. Everyone loved Little Red Riding Hood, especially her grandmother.

One day her mother told her to visit her sick grandmother.

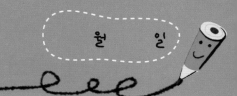

옛날에 작고 예쁜 소녀가 살았습니다.

그녀는 아름다운 숲 속 근처 작은 집에서 살았습니다.

그 소녀는 항상 빨간 모자가 달린 망토를 입고 다녀서 사람들은 그녀를 빨간 모자라고 불렀습니다.

그것은 생일 때 할머니가 주신 선물이었습니다.

모든 사람들이 빨간 모자를 좋아했고 특히 그녀의 할머니는 더욱 그녀를 사랑했습니다.

어느날 엄마는 그녀에게 아픈 할머니에게 다녀오라고 말했습니다.

"Your grandmother is sick.

Go to her house and take her this basket of some

fruits, bread and soup.

You must go straight to your grandmother's house.

Don't talk to strangers on the way."

"Yes, Mother." said Little Red Riding Hood.

She took the basket and entered the wood.

Suddenly a big wolf stepped out from behind

a tree.

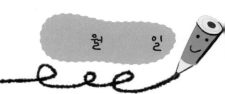
"할머니가 편찮으시단다.

할머니 댁으로 가서 과일과 빵과 수프가 들어있는 이 바구니를 전해드려라.

곧장 할머니 댁으로 가야 한다. 가는 도중에 낯선 사람과 이야기하지 말고."

"네, 엄마." 빨간 모자가 말했습니다.

그녀는 바구니를 받아들고 숲으로 들어갔습니다.

갑자기 나무 뒤에서 큰 늑대가 나왔습니다.

"Where are you going, little girl?" asked the wolf.

"I'm taking some food to my grandmother because she is sick." replied Little Red Riding Hood.

"Where does your grandmother live?"

"She lives in the old house at the end of the path in the forest."

"Does she live alone?" asked the wolf again.

"Yes. She is all alone." said Little Red Riding Hood.

'Perhaps I can eat this little girl and her grandmother.' thought the wolf.

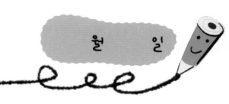

"어딜 가고 있니? 작은 소녀야?" 늑대가 물었습니다.

"할머니가 아프셔서 음식을 가져다 드리려고 가고 있어요." 빨간 모자가 대답했습니다.

"할머니가 어디에 사시는데?"

"이 길 끝에 있는 숲 속 오래된 집에서 사세요."

"할머니는 혼자 사시니?" 늑대가 다시 물었습니다.

"네, 혼자 사세요." 빨간 모자가 말했습니다.

'작은 소녀와 할머니를 잡아먹을 수 있을 것 같군.' 늑대는 생각했습니다.

The wolf walked along beside Little Red Riding Hood and said.

"If you are going to visit your sick grandmother, you should bring some flowers."

"That's a good idea. Thank you." said Little Red Riding Hood.

So she ran from the path into the wood to look for flowers.

Meanwhile the wolf ran straight to the grandmother's house and knocked on the door.

늑대는 빨간 모자를 따라 걸으면서 말했습니다.

"아프신 할머니 집에 가는 거라면 꽃이라도 가져가야 한단다."

"그거 좋은 생각이네요. 고마워요." 빨간 모자가 말했습니다.

그래서 그녀는 꽃을 찾기 위해 숲으로 들어갔습니다.

그러는 동안 늑대는 할머니의 집으로 곧장 달려가서 문을 두드렸습니다.

"Who's there?" asked the grandmother.

"It's Little Red Riding Hood, grandmother." answered the wolf, making his voice as soft as he could.

"Oh, come in sweetie."

The grandmother opened the door and was eaten by the wolf.

He put on the grandmother's clothes and hid in her bed.

When Little Red Riding Hood had gathered so many that she could carry no more, she remembered her grandmother.

She ran back to the road, and soon she came to her grandmother's house.

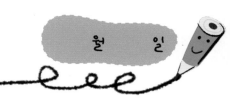

5

"누구세요?" 할머니가 물었습니다.

"빨간 모자예요, 할머니." 목소리를 최대한 부드럽게 하면서 늑대가 대답했습니다.

"오, 아가야 들어오렴."

할머니는 문을 열어주었고 늑대에게 잡아먹히고 말았습니다.

늑대는 할머니의 옷을 걸치고 할머니의 침대에 숨었습니다.

빨간 모자는 더 이상 들고 다닐 수 없을 만큼 많은 꽃을 모았을 때, 할머니가 생각이 났습니다.

그녀는 길로 돌아가서 곧 할머니 댁에 도착했습니다.

"Hello, grandmother." said Little Red Riding Hood.

"I've brought you some food, and some beautiful flowers!"

Little Red Riding Hood looked at her grandmother. "You must have been real sick. You look very strange today."

Little Red Riding Hood came closer to the bed.

"Oh, grandmother, what big ears you have!"

"All the better to hear with, my child." the wolf responded.

6

"안녕하세요, 할머니." 빨간 모자가 말했습니다.

"제가 음식을 가져왔어요. 그리고 예쁜 꽃도 가져왔어요!"

빨간 모자는 할머니를 바라보았습니다.

"할머니 많이 아프셨군요. 오늘 이상해 보여요."

빨간 모자는 침대 가까이로 다가갔습니다.

"어머 할머니, 귀가 아주 커요!"

"그건 너의 목소리를 더 잘 듣기 위해서란다. 아가야." 늑대가 대답했습니다.

"What big eyes you have!" she said.

"All the better to see with, my child."

"But grandmother, what big teeth you have!"

"All the better to eat you up with."

Before the wolf finished those words, he jumped out of bed and gobbled up Little Red Riding Hood.

He was now so full and sleepy after both Little Red Riding Hood and her grandmother.

He climbed back into the bed and fell asleep.

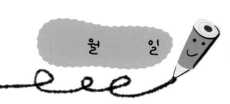

7

"눈도 아주 커요!" 그녀가 말했습니다.

"그건 너의 모습을 더 잘 보기 위해서란다. 아가야."

"하지만 할머니, 이빨도 아주 커요!"

"그건 너를 잘 잡아먹기 위해서지."

말이 끝나기도 전에 늑대는 침대에서 뛰어 나와 빨간 모자를 잡아먹었습니다.

늑대는 빨간 모자와 할머니까지 먹은 후에 배가 많이 불러서 졸음이 왔습니다.

그는 침대로 돌아가서 잠이 들었습니다.

The wolf was snoring very loudly.

A hunter passing by heard his snoring.

'I've never heard the old woman snore that loudly.'
he thought.

So the hunter went into the house.

As he entered the bedroom, he found the wolf in
grandmother's bed.

"**Oh no!** The old woman must have been eaten by
the wolf."

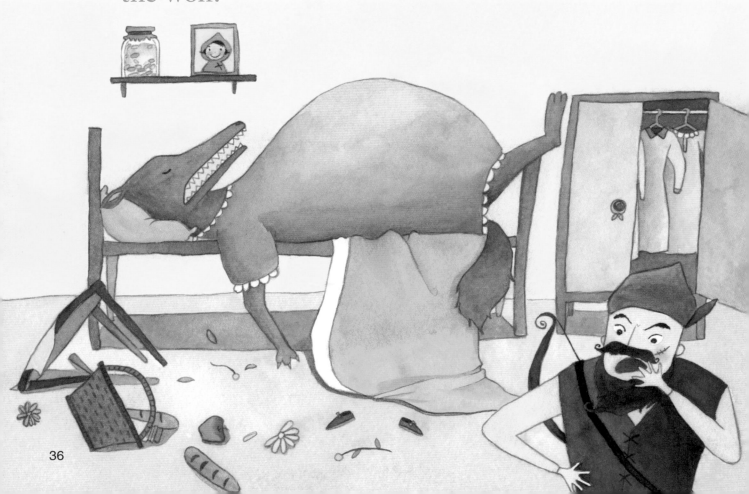

8

늦대는 아주 크게 코를 골아댔습니다.

지나가던 한 사냥꾼이 그 소리를 들었습니다.

'할머니가 이렇게 크게 코를 고는 것을 들어본 적이 없는데.' 그는 생각했습니다.

그래서 사냥꾼은 집안으로 들어갔습니다.

침실로 들어갔을 때 그는 할머니의 침대에서 늑대를 보았습니다.

"오 안돼! 할머니가 늑대에게 잡아먹힌 게 분명해."

Just then he could hear the people crying for help inside the wolf.

"Somebody, help! Somebody, help!"

The hunter cut the wolf's belly open.

Little Red Riding Hood and grandmother climbed out off the wolf.

"Thank you so much." they said.

Little Red Riding Hood ran outside and picked up lots of stones.

The hunter put them in the wolf's belly and the grandmother sewed the belly up.

9

바로 그때 그는 늑대 몸속에서 도와 달라고 소리치는 사람들의 소리를 들을 수 있었습니다.

"누가 좀 도와주세요! 누가 좀 도와주세요!"

사냥꾼은 늑대의 배를 잘라 열었습니다.

빨간 모자와 할머니가 늑대의 배에서 나왔습니다.

"정말 감사합니다." 그들이 말했습니다.

빨간 모자는 밖으로 가서 많은 돌을 모았습니다.

사냥꾼은 늑대의 배에 돌들을 넣었고 할머니가 꿰맸습니다.

Then the wolf woke up.

"I am very thirsty. I wonder why I feel so heavy."

The fat wolf went to the pond to drink water.

He bowed to drink water, but he fell in the pond.

Little Red Riding Hood, her grandmother, and
the hunter were delighted.

And Little Red Riding Hood was always careful
not to talk to any strangers.

#10

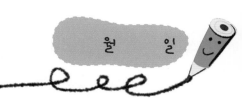

그 다음에 늑대가 깨어났습니다.

"목이 마르군. 왜 이리 몸이 무거울까?"

그 뚱뚱한 늑대는 물을 마시기 위해 연못으로 갔습니다.

그는 물을 마시기 위해 고개를 숙였고 연못에 빠졌습니다.

빨간 모자와 할머니, 그리고 사냥꾼은 기뻤습니다.

그리고 빨간 모자는 낯선 사람과는 얘기를 나누지 않고 항상 조심했답니다.

The little girl always put on a red cloak with a hood.

그 작은 소녀는 항상 빨간 모자가 달린 망토를 입었다.

그녀는 코트와 치마를 입고 나갔다.

코트 coat

그녀는 목욕을 하고 잠옷을 입었다.

잠옷 nightgown

그녀는 드레스를 입고 집에서 뛰쳐나갔다.

뛰쳐 나가다 rush out

그는 모자를 썼다.

모자 hat

She put on her coat and skirt and went out. / She bathed and put on her nightgown.
She put on a dress and rushed out of the house. / He put on a hat.

Where are you going, little girl?

작은 소녀야, 어딜 가는 중이니?

할머니는 어디 사시니?

할머니 grandmother

어디서 춤을 배웠습니까?

춤을 배우다 learn to dance

지금 어디 계신가요?

지금 present time

여기서 가장 가까운 공중전화가 어디에 있죠?

공중전화 pay phone

Where does your grandmother live? / Where did you learn to dance?
Where are you located at the present time? / Where can I find the nearest pay phone?

You must have been real sick.

당신은 많이 아픈 게 틀림없어요.

그녀는 젊었을 때 분명히 아름다웠을 것이다.

아름다운 beautiful

앞에 교통사고가 난 것이 틀림없다.

교통사고 accident

분명히 네가 뭘 잘못했을 것이다.

잘못한 wrong

그 생각에 동의하다니 내가 제정신이 아니었던 모양이다.

제정신이 아닌 insane, 동의하다 agree

She must have been beautiful when she was young.
There must have been an accident up ahead. / You must have been doing something wrong.
I must have been insane to agree to the idea.

What big ears you have!

아주 큰 귀를 가졌군요!

날씨 정말 좋구나!

날씨 weather

정말 재밌는 사람들이구나!

재미있는 interesting

남자답게 컸구나!

자라다 grow

그 녀석 목소리 한번 크구나!

목소리 voice

What beautiful weather! / What interesting people they are!
What a big boy you've grown! / What a big voice he's got!

Story 2

Cinderella

신데렐라

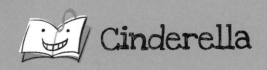 Cinderella

Track 11

1 Once upon a time there lived an unhappy young girl.

Her name is Cinderella.

Her mother died when Cinderella was young and her father found another wife.

Cinderella's stepmother already had two daughters.

She didn't like Cinderella.

Her stepmother gave Cinderella all the chores. She had to work hard all day.

Track 12

2 One day, the king threw a party and invited all the girls of the country.

Cinderella's stepsisters were going to the party.

"The Prince will probably choose a princess at the party. We have to look pretty at the party! What should we wear?"

Cinderella had to help them get dressed and brush their hair.

After the sisters left for the ball, Cinderella burst into tears.

Track 13

3 "I want to go to the party, too." She cried.

Suddenly, a fairy appeared.

"Why are you crying?"

"Because I can't go to the party."

"Don't worry. I can give you everything you want.

But first we'll need a pumpkin, four little mice, and one large lizard."

Cinderella brought the fairy what she asked for.

Track 14

4 First, the fairy struck the pumpkin with her wand.

The pumpkin disappeared, and in its place stood a beautiful coach.

Then she waved her wand.

The four little mice turned into a team of handsome carriage horses.

And the lizard became a coachman.

Cinderella could hardly believe her eyes.

Cinderella

5 The fairy even changed Cinderella's clothes into a beautiful dress and gave her a pair of glass shoes.

"You shall go to the ball, Cinderella.

But remember! You must leave the ball by midnight.

That is when my spell ends, and everything will change back to their original form." the fairy said.

6 Cinderella promised to leave by twelve o'clock.

Then she climbed up the steps into her beautiful coach.

The four white horses set off toward the king's palace.

The coach arrived at the palace, and Cinderella went into the ball.

As soon as Cinderella entered the ballroom, the Prince could not take his eyes off her.

7 "Who's she?" "I've never seen her before. She is so beautiful."

The guests were surprised and watched her.

The Prince asked Cinderella if she would like to dance.

"Will you dance with me?" "Yes, I will."

Cinderella and the Prince danced all evening.

She felt as if she was dreaming.

8 Just then she heard the clock's first stroke of midnight.

"Oh, I have to go now!"

Cinderella screamed as she ran from the palace.

"Wait!" The Prince ran after her, but it was too late.

Cinderella hurried down the stairs so fast that one of her glass shoe fell off.

The Prince found it and picked it up.

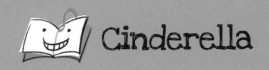
Track 19

9 He ordered his attendant to find the girl.

"Go and search everywhere for the girl whose foot fits this glass shoe."

So the attendant went to every house in the kingdom, and soon he came to Cinderella's house.

"Will you try on this shoe?"

The attendant first asked her stepsisters to try on the shoe.

But it didn't fit any of their feet.

10 "Are there any other girls in the house?" asked the attendant.

"Can I try it on?" said Cinderella.

"Of course, you can." he replied.

So Cinderella came forward to try on the glass shoe.

It fit perfectly. Everyone was shocked.

"And I have the other one." said Cinderella.

Cinderella and the prince got married, and they lived happily ever after.

die die die die die die die die
죽다

daughter daughter daughter daughter
딸

chore chore chore chore chore chore
일

invite invite invite invite invite invite
초대하다

stepsister stepsister stepsister stepsister
의붓 자매

prince prince prince prince prince prince

왕자

wear wear wear wear wear wear wear

입다

brush brush brush brush brush brush

솔질하다

ball ball ball ball ball ball ball

무도회

burst burst burst burst burst burst

터뜨리다

fairy fairy fairy fairy fairy fairy fairy

요정

appear appear appear appear appear

나타나다

pumpkin pumpkin pumpkin pumpkin

호박

lizard lizard lizard lizard lizard lizard

도마뱀

wand wand wand wand wand wand

지팡이

disappear disappear disappear disappear

사라지다

coach coach coach coach coach coach

마차

carriage carriage carriage carriage

운반

coachman coachman coachman coachman

마부

remember remember remember remember

기억하다

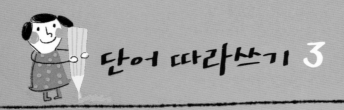
midnight　 midnight　 midnight　 midnight

자정

spell　 spell　 spell　 spell　 spell　 spell　 spell

주문

promise　 promise　 promise　 promise　 promise

약속하다

palace　 palace　 palace　 palace　 palace

궁전

dance　 dance　 dance　 dance　 dance　 dance

춤추다

stroke stroke stroke stroke stroke stroke

치기, 때리기

scream scream scream scream scream

비명을 지르다

attendant attendant attendant attendant

시종

search search search search search search

찾다

perfectly perfectly perfectly perfectly

완벽하게

Cinderella

신데렐라

Once upon a time there lived an unhappy young girl.

Her name is Cinderella.

Her mother died when Cinderella was young and her father found another wife.

Cinderella's stepmother already had two daughters.

She didn't like Cinderella.

Her stepmother gave Cinderella all the chores.

She had to work hard all day.

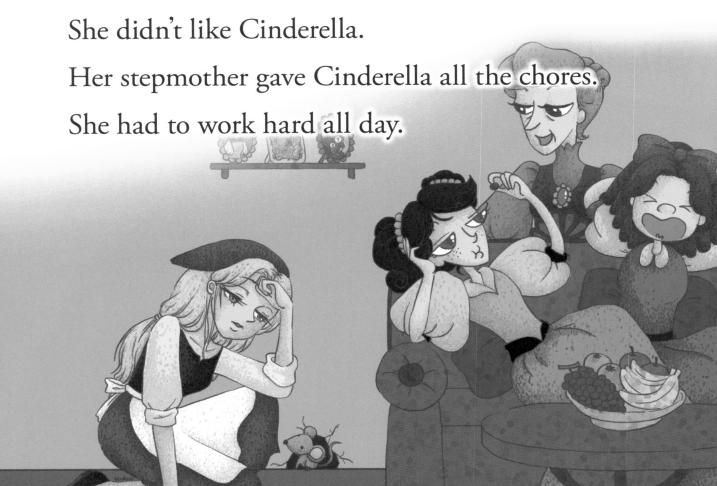

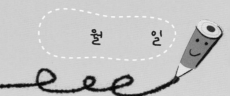

옛날 불행한 한 소녀가 살았습니다.

그녀의 이름은 신데렐라였습니다.

그녀의 어머니는 세상을 떠났고 그녀의 아버지는 새로운 부인을 맞이했습니다.

신데렐라의 새엄마에게는 이미 두 딸이 있었습니다.

그녀는 신데렐라를 싫어했습니다.

새엄마는 신데렐라에게 집안의 모든 일을 시켰습니다.

그녀는 하루종일 일해야 했습니다.

One day, the king threw a party and invited all the girls of the country.

Cinderella's stepsisters were going to the party.

"The Prince will probably choose a princess at the party. We have to look pretty at the party! What should we wear?"

Cinderella had to help them get dressed and brush their hair.

After the sisters left for the ball, Cinderella burst into tears.

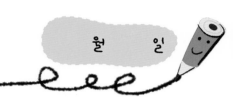

2

어느날 왕이 파티를 열었고 온 나라의 아가씨들을 초대했습니다.

신데렐라의 의붓자매들은 파티에 가려고 준비했습니다.

"왕자가 파티에서 공주를 고를 거야. 우리는 파티에서 예뻐 보여야 해! 무슨 옷을 입을까?"

신데렐라는 그녀들이 옷을 입는 것을 도와주고 그녀들의 머리를 빗겨주어야 했습니다.

그녀들이 무도회로 떠났을 때 신데렐라는 울음을 터뜨렸습니다.

"I want to go to the party, too." She cried.

Suddenly, a fairy appeared.

"Why are you crying?"

"Because I can't go to the party."

"Don't worry. I can give you everything you want.

But first we'll need a pumpkin, four little mice,

and one large lizard."

Cinderella brought the fairy what she asked for.

3

"나도 파티에 가고 싶어." 그녀는 울었습니다.

갑자기 요정이 나타났습니다.

"왜 울고 있니?"

"저는 파티에 갈 수가 없기 때문에요."

"걱정 마라. 내가 너를 위해 무엇이든지 해줄 수 있단다.

그러나 먼저 우리는 호박 한 개, 네 마리의 생쥐와 큰 도마뱀 한 마리가 필요하단다."

신데렐라는 요정이 말한 것들을 가져왔습니다.

First, the fairy struck the pumpkin with her wand.

The pumpkin disappeared, and in its place stood a

beautiful coach.

Then she waved her wand.

The four little mice turned into a team of handsome

carriage horses.

And the lizard became a coachman.

Cinderella could hardly believe her eyes.

4

요정이 그녀의 지팡이로 호박을 쳤습니다.

호박은 사라지고 아름다운 마차가 그 자리에 서 있었습니다.

그러고 나서 그녀는 지팡이를 흔들었습니다.

네 마리의 생쥐는 잘생긴 한 팀의 마차 말들로 변했습니다.

그리고 도마뱀은 마부로 변했습니다.

신데렐라는 자신이 본 것을 믿을 수가 없었습니다.

The fairy even changed Cinderella's clothes into a
beautiful dress and gave her a pair of glass shoes.
"You shall go to the ball, Cinderella.
But remember!
You must leave the ball by midnight.
That is when my spell ends, and everything will
change back to their original form." the fairy said.

요정은 신데렐라의 옷을 아름다운 드레스로 바꾸어 주었고 한 쌍의 유리 구두를 주었습니다.

"너는 이제 무도회에 갈 수 있단다, 신데렐라.

하지만 명심해라!

너는 밤 12시에 무도회에서 떠나야만 한단다.

그때 내 마법이 사라져서 원래의 모습으로 돌아간단다." 요정이 말했습니다.

Cinderella promised to leave by twelve o'clock.

Then she climbed up the steps into her beautiful coach.

The four white horses set off toward the king's palace.

The coach arrived at the palace, and Cinderella went into the ball.

As soon as Cinderella entered the ballroom, the Prince could not take his eyes off her.

신데렐라는 12시까지 돌아오겠다고 약속했습니다.

그리고 나서 그녀는 아름다운 마차에 올라탔습니다.

네 마리의 말은 왕의 궁전으로 출발했습니다.

마차가 궁전에 도착했고 신데렐라는 무도회에 갔습니다.

신데렐라가 무도회장에 들어서자 왕자는 그녀에게서 눈을 뗄 수가 없었습니다.

"Who's she?"

"I've never seen her before. She is so beautiful."

The guests were surprised and watched her.

The Prince asked Cinderella if she would like to dance.

"Will you dance with me?"

"Yes, I will."

Cinderella and the Prince danced all evening.

She felt as if she was dreaming.

"누구지?"

"본 적이 없는 얼굴인데. 정말 아름답네."

손님들도 놀라서 그녀를 바라보았습니다.

왕자가 신데렐라에게 춤을 추겠냐고 물어보았습니다.

"저와 춤추시겠어요?"

"네, 좋아요."

신데렐라와 왕자는 저녁 내내 춤을 추었습니다.

그녀는 마치 꿈을 꾸는 것 같았습니다.

Just then she heard the clock's first stroke of midnight.

"Oh, I have to go now!"

Cinderella screamed as she ran from the palace.

"Wait!" The Prince ran after her, but it was too late.

Cinderella hurried down the stairs so fast that one of her glass shoe fell off.

The Prince found it and picked it up.

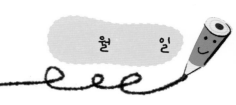

8

그때 그녀는 자정을 알리는 첫 번째 종소리를 들었습니다.

"오, 난 지금 가야 해요!"

신데렐라는 소리치며 궁전에서 도망쳤습니다.

"기다려요!" 왕자가 뒤쫓았지만 너무 늦었습니다.

신데렐라는 서둘러 계단을 내려왔고 유리 구두 한 짝이 벗겨졌습니다.

왕자가 구두를 발견하고 집어들었습니다.

He ordered his attendant to find the girl.

"Go and search everywhere for the girl whose foot fits this glass shoe."

So the attendant went to every house in the kingdom, and soon he came to Cinderella's house.

"Will you try on this shoe?"

The attendant first asked her stepsisters to try on the shoe.

But it didn't fit any of their feet.

9

그는 시종에게 그 소녀를 찾으라고 명령했습니다.

"가서 모든 곳을 뒤져서 이 신발이 맞는 아가씨를 찾아라."

그래서 시종은 왕국의 모든 집을 들렀고 곧 신데렐라의 집으로 왔습니다.

"이 신발을 신어 보시겠어요?"

시종은 처음에 신데렐라의 의붓언니들에게 신발을 신어보기를 권했습니다.

그러나 그 신발은 그녀들의 발에는 전혀 맞지 않았습니다.

"Are there any other girls in the house?" asked the attendant.

"Can I try it on?" said Cinderella.

"Of course, you can." he replied.

So Cinderella came forward to try on the glass shoe.

It fit perfectly. Everyone was shocked.

"And I have the other one." said Cinderella.

Cinderella and the prince got married, and they lived happily ever after.

10

"이 집에 다른 아가씨는 없나요?" 시종이 물었습니다.

"제가 신어봐도 될까요?" 신데렐라가 말했습니다.

"물론이죠. 신어보세요." 그는 대답했습니다.

신데렐라는 유리 구두를 신기 위해 앞으로 나갔습니다.

구두는 완벽하게 맞았습니다. 모두들 놀랐습니다.

"제가 다른 한쪽도 가지고 있어요." 신데렐라가 말했습니다.

신데렐라와 왕자는 결혼을 했고, 이후로 행복하게 살았습니다.

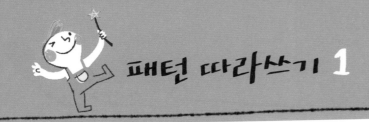

The stepsisters were going to the party.

의붓 언니들은 그 파티에 가려고 했다.

오늘 오후에는 맑을 것이다.

오후 afternoon

그녀는 내년에 15살이 된다.

내년 next year

그 과제가 언제 끝날지 모르겠다.

끝나다 be over

이번 여름방학에는 해변가에 갈 예정이다.

여름 방학 summer vacation

It is going to be sunny in the afternoon today. / She is going to be 15 next year.
I don't know when the homework is going to be over.
I'll be going to the beach this summer vacation.

Cinderella brought what the fairy asked.

신데렐라는 요정이 요청한 것을 가져왔다.

그는 먹는 것을 아주 가린다.

가리는 choosy

내 말은 그런 뜻이 아니었다.

의미하다 mean

정확히 무슨 일이 일어났는지 아니?

일어나다 happen

남들이 나에 대해서 뭐라고 하든 나는 신경쓰지 않는다.

사람들 people

He is very choosy about what he eats. / That was not what I mean.
Do you know exactly what happened? / I don't mind what people say of me.

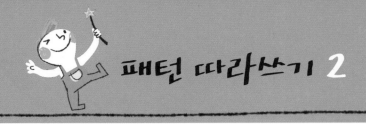

The four little mice turned into a team of handsome carriage horses.

네 마리의 생쥐는 잘생긴 한 팀의 마차 말들로 변했다.

그 지역은 폐허로 변해 버렸다.

폐허 ruins

우리가 꿈꾸던 휴가가 악몽으로 변했다.

휴가 holiday, 악몽 nightmare

오래된 기차역이 박물관으로 바뀌었다.

박물관 museum

우유는 치즈나 요구르트로 변한다.

요구르트 yogurt

The area turned into ruins. / Our dream holiday turned into a nightmare.
The old train station has been turned into a museum. / Milk turn into cheese or yogurt.

Will you dance with me?

저와 춤추시겠어요?

설거지 좀 해줄래요?

설거지 하다 do the dishes

부탁 하나 해도 될까요?

호의, 친절 favor

이 문제를 풀도록 도와주시겠어요?

문제 problem

그 도서관까지 저랑 같이 걸어 갈래요?

도서관 library

Will you please do the dishes? / Will you do me a favor?
Will you help me to do this problem? / Will you walk down to the library with me?

My
Book
report

나만의 독서록 쓰기

Little Red Riding Hood

Choose one character from the story and write about him or her. 이야기에 등장하는 한 인물을 골라서 그 인물에 대해 써 보세요.

신체적특징

인물의 성격

인물에게 하고싶은 말

Cinderella

Choose one character from the story and write about him or her. 이야기에 등장하는 한 인물을 골라서 그 인물에 대해 써 보세요.

신체적특징

인물의 성격

인물에게 하고싶은 말

Little Red Riding Hood

Create a cartoon that explains the book you read.

읽은 책의 내용을 설명할 수 있는 만화를 그려보세요.

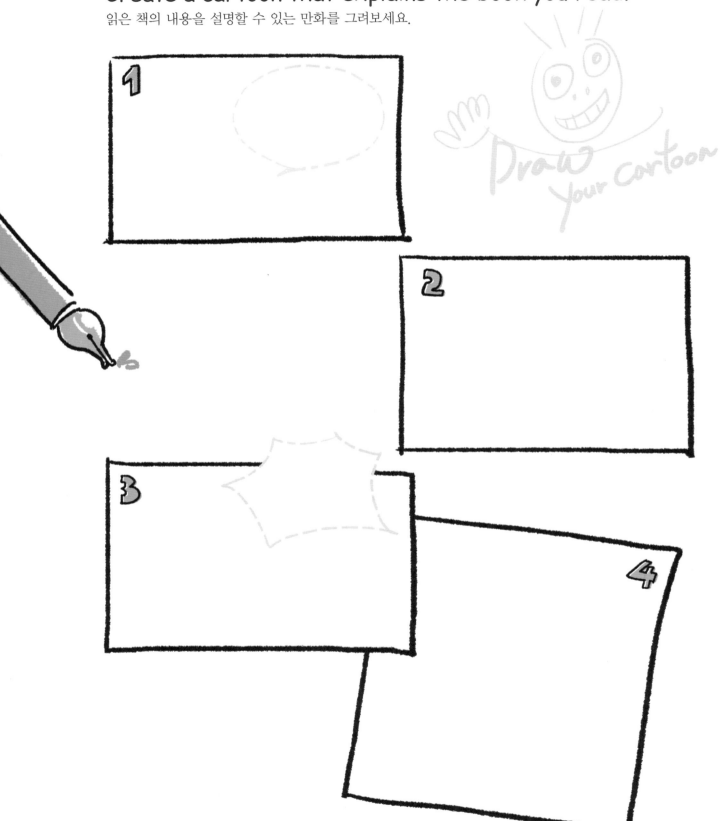

Cinderella

Create a cartoon that explains the book you read.
읽은 책의 내용을 설명할 수 있는 만화를 그려보세요.

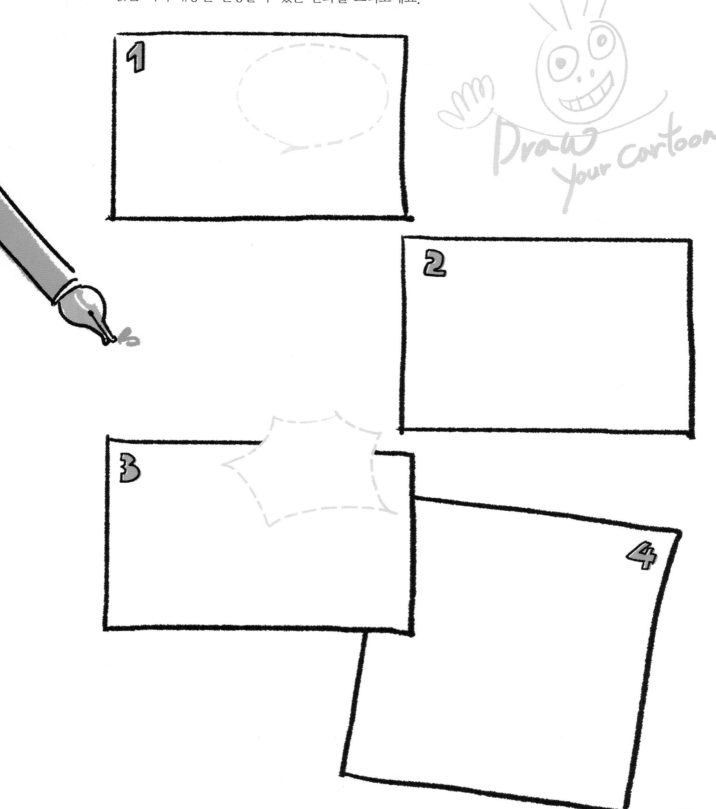

Draw your cartoon

 Little Red Riding Hood

Write a short summary of the story.
이야기의 요약을 간단하게 써보세요.

 Cinderella

Write a short summary of the story.
이야기의 요약을 간단하게 써보세요.

 Little Red Riding Hood

Imagine that you are a reporter and interview one of the characters from the story.
기자가 되었다고 생각하고 이야기 속 주인공 중 한 명을 골라 인터뷰를 해 보세요.

DATE

 Cinderella

 Imagine that you are a reporter and interview one of the characters from the story.
기자가 되었다고 생각하고 이야기 속 주인공 중 한 명을 골라 인터뷰를 해 보세요.

DATE

Imagine that you are a character from the story and write a diary.
책 속의 주인공 중 한 명이 자기의 모습이라고 생각하고 일기를 써 보세요.

DATE

 Cinderella

Imagine that you are a character from the story and write a diary.
책 속의 주인공 중 한 명이 자기의 모습이라고 생각하고 일기를 써 보세요.

DATE

Memo

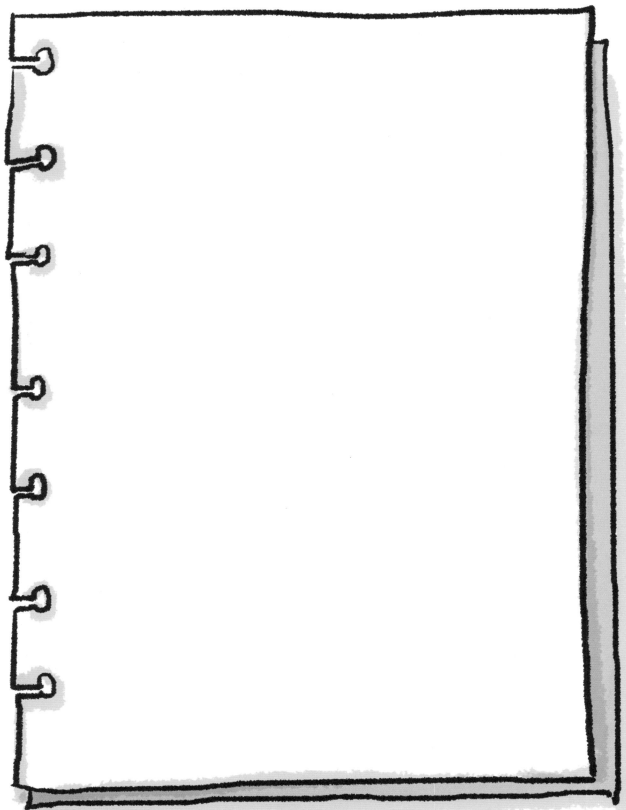